Children of
IRELAND

THE WORLD'S CHILDREN

Children of IRELAND

MICHAEL ELSOHN ROSS
PHOTOGRAPHS BY FELIX RIGAU

Carolrhoda Books, Inc./Minneapolis

To Nick and Cait, and to all the other children who made this book possible   —M.E.R. and F.R.

We would like to express our sincere gratitude to the McGinley family for their kindness and generosity in helping us write and edit this book.   —M.E.R. and F.R.

Text copyright © 2002 by Michael Elsohn Ross
Photographs copyright © 2002 by Felix Rigau

Carolrhoda Books, Inc.
A division of Lerner Publishing Group
241 First Avenue North
Minneapolis, MN 55401 U.S.A.

Website address: www.lernerbooks.com

Library of Congress Cataloging-in-Publication Data

Ross, Michael Elsohn, 1952–
    Children of Ireland / Michael Elsohn Ross ; photographs by Felix Rigau.
        p.   cm. — (The world's children)
    Includes index.
    ISBN: 1–57505–521–X (lib. bdg. : alk. paper)
    1. Ireland—Juvenile literature. 2. Children—Ireland—Juvenile literature. [1. Ireland—Social life and customs.] I. Rigau, Felix, ill. II. Title. III. World's children (Minneapolis, Minn.)
    DA906.R67 2002
    941.5—dc21   00–012107

Manufactured in the United States of America
1 2 3 4 5 6 – JR – 07 06 05 04 03 02

From his front door, John can watch the fishing boats in Castlemaine Harbor. Like most children in Ireland, he lives near the sea. Ireland is an island with almost 2,000 miles of coast. The Republic of Ireland, the country where John lives, covers most of the island and is a little bigger than the state of West Virginia. John's home is in the village of Cromane on the southwestern coast.

John finds it hard to imagine a better life than one on the seashore. He hopes to work on a fishing boat someday.

The sea has always played an important part in Ireland's history. For thousands of years, people have crossed it to explore and settle here. People called Celts came from eastern Europe more than 2,000 years ago. Much of Irish music, art, and language are still based on Celtic culture. Then, beginning around the 200s, missionaries brought the Roman Catholic religion to Ireland. One of the most famous was Saint Patrick, who preached in Ireland during the 400s.

The sea has brought thousands of visitors—both friendly and unfriendly—to Ireland's shore.

The Celts and missionaries were only the beginning. A few hundred years later, Vikings invaded Ireland, followed by Normans from England. Over time, the English took over the country. They took Irish land away from farmers and banned Irish culture and the Catholic religion. The Irish fought back and kept their language, art, and religion alive in secret. But for centuries, Ireland remained under English control. The island eventually became part of a nation called the United Kingdom of Great Britain and Ireland.

Irish soldiers defended this castle against English armies until it was destroyed in the 1640s.

The Irish didn't give up their dream of regaining their land and their freedom. Finally, in 1921, the British and the Irish agreed to divide the island of Ireland in two. In the southern and western parts of the island, most people considered themselves Irish. This area eventually became the Republic of Ireland. In the north, many people considered themselves British. This area remained under British control and became known as the nation of Northern Ireland.

Ireland is divided into 26 counties. About 3,700,000 people live there.

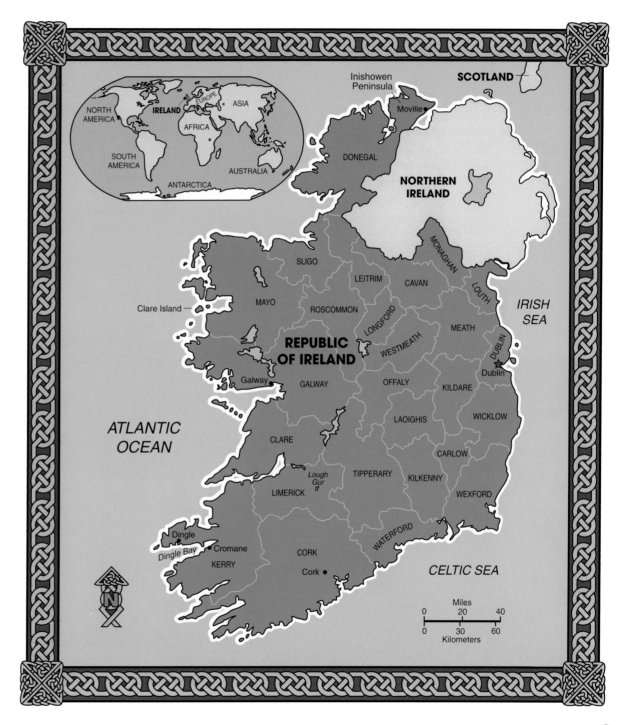

9

John and his friends sort mussels to earn spending money. John's earnings pay for bus rides to track meets, where he hurdles and runs races.

John has learned about his country's history in school, but during summer vacation, he's more concerned about earning spending money. On weekends, John, his brothers, and their friends clean and sort mussels. Mussels are a type of shellfish. They grow underwater on metal grates in the harbor. Fishers harvest the mussels and load them into a sorting machine, which shoots the large ones onto a tray. The boys toss out empty shells and drop the whole mussels into sacks. They must work quickly and carefully. The sorter is noisy, but the boys still have a good time chatting and laughing.

For extra cash, the boys also visit the bogs, or marshy areas, near town to cut chunks of peat. Peat is made up of partly rotted plants. It forms when plants die in soggy places and the moisture keeps them from decaying entirely. Dried peat can be burned in stoves or fireplaces. Many Irish homes are heated this way.

Ireland's peat bogs have slowly grown over thousands of years. Some are more than 40 feet deep. But as the country's population increases, people are cutting more and more peat. Bogs are also being drained and turned into farmland. Some people are trying to save the bogs before they all disappear.

These chunks of peat are ready to be dried and burned to heat homes.

Jessica lives across Dingle Bay in the fishing village of Dingle. A colorful collection of fishing boats sits in the harbor. Jessica's father is the captain of a large boat called a trawler, which uses a big net to catch fish. Jessica is too young to go out to sea with her father, but she and her little sister, Rebecca, often come aboard his boat. They are comfortable climbing off the wharf onto the boat, even though it rocks back and forth with the waves.

Jessica and Rebecca visit the Resolution II *with their father, Michael. Some of Michael's fishing trips last 10 days or more, but he can call the girls from the boat's telephone.*

Fishing has been an important occupation in Ireland for centuries. But fishers like Jessica's father are concerned about the future. Each year so many fish are caught that in many parts of the world, there are fewer to catch the following year. Tourism is becoming a bigger industry in towns like Dingle. Perhaps when Jessica and her friends are adults, more people in Dingle will make their living from visitors than from the sea.

Brightly colored boats make Dingle's harbor a cheerful place.

Jessica practices speaking Gaelic with her teacher. The day's lesson is written on the poster behind them.

Jessica's school sits atop a hill overlooking the harbor. Like most schools in Ireland, it's operated by the Catholic Church. More than nine out of ten Irish are Catholic, and the Church affects many parts of people's lives. Most of Jessica's teachers are nuns, women who dedicate their lives to serving the Church. Each day at school, Jessica and her classmates have a half hour of religious instruction.

Besides religion, English, and other subjects, Irish schoolchildren also learn Gaelic, the Irish language. During the centuries that Britain ruled Ireland, this ancient language almost disappeared. English is still the country's main spoken language. But Gaelic is also an official language, and many people want to preserve it. So children are required to learn it in school.

Like most students, Jessica wears a school uniform. Since her school is in the center of town, it has a small paved yard to play in instead of a grassy field. During recess, Jessica hula hoops or jumps rope. At lunch, the children are free to go into town or home for lunch. Jessica often walks down the street to a shop, where she buys chips, or french fries.

School uniforms are required in almost every Irish school.

The Red Abbey tower (left) is one of the oldest buildings in Cork. It stands near St. Killian's School (right).

Valerie and Elizabeth go to St. Killian's School in Cork. From the school, they can see the Red Abbey. In 1690, during one of many Irish uprisings against the English, the abbey was used in an important battle. Back then, the abbey was outside the city's walls, so English troops set up a cannon there to bombard the city. Eventually the English secured their power over Cork and the rest of Ireland. Then they passed new laws that denied Irish Catholics many rights, including the rights to buy land and to teach their children Irish culture.

Elizabeth and Valerie visit Sister Rosario.

Next door to St. Killian's is the South Presentation Convent. A convent is a community of nuns. South Presentation was founded in 1775 by a nun named Nano Nagle. Nano became famous for her work establishing Catholic schools for poor children at a time when such schools were against English law. She is buried in the graveyard next to a small museum, where her old books and other relics are displayed.

This memorial to Nano Nagle honors her courage in opening Catholic schools at a time when the English had made Catholic education a crime punishable by death.

Above: *Sister Rosario lovingly tends the graveyard where Nano Nagle is buried.* Left: *The school's grounds are one of the most peaceful places in Cork, Ireland's second-largest city.*

Though the battles with the English happened long ago, the people of Cork have not forgotten them. Elizabeth knows about the siege of her city and Nano Nagle's work. She thinks that if she had lived during the days of the English invasions, she could have taken care of herself. Twice a week she takes karate lessons, and she hopes to earn her brown belt this summer.

County Cork is a center for Irish sports that have been played for thousands of years, such as hurling. Though hurling was banned by the English, it survived and is played by many modern Irish. Using a flat, curved stick called a hurley, players hit, carry, or drive the ball along the ground. A hurley ball is called a *sliotar* and is about the size of a baseball, with raised ridges. A player scores a goal by sending the sliotar between the opposing team's goalposts.

Cormac and Eoghan have played hurling since they were five years old. It's a rough sport. During one practice, Eoghan gets hit and takes a short time-out to recover from the blow. The boys' friend Dave once broke his hand in a hurling match. Despite the danger, Cormac and Eoghan think the game is well worth playing. Last year, Eoghan's team went to the national finals for their age group. They lost the championship to a team from Galway, but both boys have high hopes for this year.

Opposite page: *Eoghan clutches his hurley, ready for the next play.* Right: *Eoghan and Dave jostle each other to reach the sliotar.* Below: *Cormac drives the sliotar toward the goal.*

Rounders is a popular game that was brought to Ireland by the English. It is so similar to baseball that some historians think it may have been the inspiration for that sport. Like baseball, rounders has outfielders, infielders, a batter, and a pitcher—but these positions have different names. Patricia plays catcher, or backstop. Her friend Katrina plays second base, or second post.

Katrina (above) *watches as Patricia* (left) *takes a swing.*

Patricia, Katrina, and their teammates from Scoil Ballinora have gone to a town near Cork to play another girls' team. (The word *scoil* means "school.") Rounders has been an official sport at Scoil Ballinora for only three years, so Patricia is glad to have a chance to play. Even when the season is over, she still practices in her yard at home.

After a pep talk, the Scoil Ballinora rounders team is eager for victory.

23

Swimming is another favorite pastime for many Irish children. Though the water is very cold along the coast of county Donegal, it doesn't stop Cait from swimming. Her fingers start to turn blue, but she keeps playing in the water. There are many beautiful beaches near Cait's town of Moville. In the evening, she and her brothers and sister often go to the shore with their parents to watch the sunset or to wave to passing ships.

This sandy beach near the village of Falcarragh in county Donegal is a good place for a stroll.

After a chilly swim, a blanket helps Cait warm up.

Rich farmland covers about two-thirds of Ireland, and farming has been an important way of life for hundreds of years.

About 150 years ago, the ships that sailed from Ireland were filled with people desperate for a better life. During the 1840s, a great famine, or food shortage, killed a million Irish. At least a million more left the country. The famine was caused by a disease called potato blight, which wiped out the potato crops that poor farm families depended on. Many of Cait's ancestors left during this time. Some never returned.

This ruined cottage dates back to the time of the potato famine. It was probably the home of a family who died or left Ireland.

Cait and her five siblings have learned about their family's history from their father, who explores it as a hobby. One ancestor, Cahir O'Doherty, was a chieftain, or Irish lord. Cahir was the last chieftain of Inishowen, the peninsula where Moville is located. (A peninsula is a point of land surrounded by water on three sides.) Cait says it's fun to play at Green Castle, the remains of a fortress where the O'Dohertys once lived. But she wouldn't want to live there—it would be much too cold and damp.

Far right: *Cait, her brothers and sister, and their parents visit Green Castle.* Right: *The castle was built in 1305. Only a few walls have survived the centuries since then.*

Malin Head, the tip of the Inishowen Peninsula, is the northernmost point in Ireland.

Another branch of the family, the McSweeneys, once lived at Doe Castle on the other side of Inishowen. Torlogh McSweeney was a well-known piper and singer. After he lost his lands to the English, he traveled around Ireland playing his music. Cait's great-grandfather was an excellent singer who was thought to have inherited his musical ability from the McSweeneys.

Like her ancestors, Cait likes to sing and play music. She takes piano and tin whistle lessons and also plays violin. Sometimes Cait performs at a local pub, a place where people gather to eat, drink, talk, and listen to music. Cait's tin whistle teacher, Kevin, plays the Irish flute while she accompanies with her whistle. Other musicians may join in on mandolin, fiddle, or guitar.

At 12 years of age, Cait easily keeps up with her adult partners—but she can't stay out as late as they do. Musical sessions like these are performed in pubs all over the country. While young players like Cait are welcome, they're usually not allowed in city pubs at night.

Cait plays at the local pub with her teacher, Kevin, and their friend Daniel. Music sessions like this one aren't formal shows. They're just a chance for friends to enjoy playing together.

A tin whistle sounds similar to a flute but is easier to learn.

In her spare time, Cait has been e-mailing a friend in California for a couple of years. Nick shares her interests in music, books, and soccer. This week he's visiting Cait for the first time. They've tried playing some music together but don't know many of the same tunes. Playing soccer with Nick and her brothers has been a bit easier. Called "football" in Ireland, soccer is a very popular sport. Children play it everywhere, from school fields to alleys.

The driveway in front of Cait's house serves as a soccer field for the children.

Southwest of Cait's home, in county Mayo, Gerard spends almost every summer day on the Atlantic Ocean. He helps his father ferry passengers from the mainland to Clare Island. Although he isn't old enough to run the ferry, his father sometimes lets him pilot the vessel when no passengers are aboard. Gerard's days are long—from eight in the morning to ten at night. But working on the ferry gives him a chance to meet visitors from all over the world.

Gerard (left) *and his father's ferry, the* Ocean Star (above)

As the ferry nears Clare Island, Gerard can see an old castle that was once a stronghold of the pirate queen Granuaile O'Malley. More than 400 years ago, Granuaile ruled parts of Ireland's western coast. The English couldn't capture her or keep her from raiding passing ships. Like many people on Clare Island, Gerard can trace his ancestry to the pirate queen.

Clare Island is one of hundreds of small islands on Ireland's coast. Many are inhabited. Before the potato famine, about 1,600 people lived on Clare Island. But in modern times, the population is only about 160. Because so few people live on the island, it has no school for children Gerard's age. After summer vacation, he'll go to school on the mainland. Then he'll come home only on weekends and holidays.

Granuaile O'Malley is said to be buried in the old abbey near her castle on Clare Island.

Gerard's friend Ian runs his own business renting bicycles to tourists. Several years ago, when Ian was 12, he opened the bike shop with his brother Niall. The shop is housed in an old shed near the pier. It doesn't look like much, but Ian has plans to fix it up. The boys use a computer to keep track of their expenses and income. When the bikes need repairs, the boys do the work themselves. On Clare Island, most teenagers work hard and are treated with the same respect given to adults. Ian was surprised when a neighbor opened a competing bike-rental shop, but he's taking the challenge in stride. He already has ideas about attracting the tourists to his shop just as they get off the ferry.

Above left: *Ian discusses the price of bike rentals with a customer.*
Left: *Ian in front of his shop*

Bicycling and walking are the best ways to get around on the island, which has few roads suitable for cars.

About one-fourth of Ireland's people live in or near Dublin, the nation's largest city. Many families live just outside the city and travel downtown to their jobs. The children, like many in Ireland, often go to schools and day-care centers while their parents work. At St. Stephen's Green, a park in downtown Dublin, children from a Montessori school play ring-around-the-rosy among the grass and trees. The green is a wonderful place to play on sunny days. As the children run about, their teachers keep a careful eye on them so that they don't get lost.

Amy's home is not far from the green. It's a row house where her family has lived for generations. These old brick homes are joined with the houses on either side. Many families live on Amy's street, and she has at least 20 cousins in the neighborhood. Her aunt Martina, who takes care of her during the day, often brings Amy's cousin Jodi to play. Sometimes the girls visit the doll shop down the street or pretend that they are princesses living in a castle.

For a special treat, Aunt Martina takes Amy and Jodi to see a real castle right in Dublin. Dublin Castle was built by King John of England almost 800 years ago. For years, the castle was the home of viceroys, British leaders who governed Ireland. In modern times, it's used for government ceremonies.

Left: *Amy outside her home in Dublin.* Below left: *A tea party at the doll shop down the street from Amy's house*

Zöe Mae and Tommie live very differently than most Irish children. They travel all over Ireland, visiting forts, tombs, and other old places.

Zöe Mae and Tommie's parents are archaeologists, scientists who study ancient cultures. People have lived in Ireland for about 8,000 years, and the country is filled with fascinating ruins that contain clues about how they lived.

Zöe Mae and Tommie take a walking trip with their parents in county Kerry.

Left: *Tommie studies the marks on an Ogham stone.* Below: *Ogham was a secret language in ancient Ireland. Few people learned how to read and write it.*

At an old burial ground on a farm in county Kerry, Tommie and Zöe Mae look for such clues. The children discover nine blocks of sandstone. Each one has lines cut into the surface. Tommie carefully counts the number of lines on each stone. He's a good counter, but he hasn't learned to read much yet—especially not the special marks carved on the rocks. These lines are a very old alphabet that people used more than 1,300 years ago. Called Ogham, the letters are made up of notched strokes that branch out from a central line. Tommie's parents say that the carvings tell the names of important people who were buried here.

Another interesting ancient site is the Grange Stone Circle in county Limerick. Ireland has many stone circles, but this one is the largest. It was built more than 4,000 years ago by people who lived around the shores of Lough Gur. (The world *lough* means "lake.") The circle is made of 113 large stones set upright and ringed by a bank of earth, grass, and smaller stones. Modern people didn't know the circle existed until 1929, when an archaeologist uncovered it.

Archaeologists think that the people who built the stone circle also brought metal tools and possibly horses to the area.

As other archaeologists explored the area, they discovered that the circle's builders were farmers who planted crops, herded animals, and hunted. Why would these people build the circle? Mystery still surrounds this place. Archaeologists think it was used for religious ceremonies. Many people say that fairies live there, too.

Daniel knows that the stone circle is a special place, but he's never seen any fairies. He and his two sisters, Katie and Annie, live across the road and sometimes play tag in the circle. Most of their friends from school live far away, so the children are lucky they enjoy each other's company.

Daniel and his sisters often play in the stone circle. Sometimes they meet other children whose parents have brought them to visit the site.

Two sheep owned by Daniel's family graze in the circle.

Like the people who lived here long ago, Daniel's family raises livestock and grows food. Daniel, the oldest child, counts the calves every day when he comes home from school. Last summer he helped milk the cows, which was a lot of work. He also keeps track of the sheep, John and Alice, who often graze in the circle.

Daniel says farm life requires a lot of responsibility.

One day, he forgot to put the hens in their coop before the family went to church. While they were gone, a fox came along and killed all of the chickens.

Katie and Annie feed a calf.

*John, the video man,
helps the children
choose movies to rent.*

Even though Daniel lives near an ancient site, in some ways his life is very modern. Every Tuesday, the video man, John, stops by with movies for rent. The children take turns picking out one movie with John's help. He not only gives reviews but also lets the kids know which films are best for kids. Many of their favorites are American films.

For Daniel and his sisters, it's easy to have a sense of history. They live on an old farm, next to an ancient historical treasure. They hear stories about the old days but are also very much aware of the world beyond Ireland. Like Daniel, Katie, and Annie, the children of Ireland are proud of their past and excited about their future.

Every day on the farm provides new chances for the children to work, play, and enjoy growing up in Ireland.

Pronunciation Guide

Cahir   KA-heer
Cait   KOTCH
Celtic   KEL-tik
Eoghan   OH-ehn
Gaelic   GAY-lik
Granuaile   GRAHN-yuh
Lough Gur   LAHK GUHR
Ogham   OH-ehm
scoil   SKUHL
sliotar   SLIH-tuhr
Torlogh   TOHR-lahk
Zöe   ZOH-ee

Index